My Life in Lists

My Life in Lists

An Illustrated Journal
to Record Your
Loves, Goals + Dreams!

NICOLE BARLETTANO

ROCK POINT

Inspiring | Educating | Creating | Entertaining

Brimming with creative inspiration, how-to projects, and useful information to enrich your everyday life, Quarto Knows is a favorite destination for those pursuing their interests and passions. Visit our site and dig deeper with our books into your area of interest: Quarto Creates, Quarto Cooks, Quarto Homes, Quarto Lives, Quarto Drives, Quarto Explores, Quarto Gifts, or Quarto Kids.

ISBN: 978-1-63106-613-9

Editorial Director: Rage Kindelsperger
Creative Director: Laura Drew
Layout: Kim Winscher
Managing Editor: Cara Donaldson
Senior Editor: Erin Canning

Printed in China

MIX
Paper from responsible sources
FSC® C008047

For

Charlotte

Contents

Lists about Your Past

Lists to Plan Your Future

Introduction

Well, hello there, my darlings! If you are anything like me, you chose this book because you are a lover of lists, and I've created this illustrated journal just for you. While making lists is a simple and common practice, they can be so much more valuable if you push them a step further. Here's how list-making (and this book) can be beneficial for you.

💜 List-making can help you focus, by taking tasks out of your head and putting them onto paper.

💜 List-making can be a therapeutic exercise, by taking pause, prioritizing, and organizing.

💜 This book is a diary, a place where you are free to express yourself and jot down your innermost feelings.

💜 This book is a time capsule, a place where you can store all your favorite things and most cherished memories.

💜 This book is a to-do list, a place where you can organize your tasks and become your most productive self.

💜 This book is a self-exploration journal, a place where you are encouraged to dig a little deeper, learn a little more, and become a better version of yourself.

Are you ready? This is your autobiography. Welcome to *My Life in Lists*.

A Little Something about Me

- I have been in love with lists for as long as I can remember.

- Even as a child, I recognized the importance of list-making and applied it to all areas of my life.

- I view this hobby as a way of maintaining my own personal external hard drive . . . on paper!

- As a busy working mother, my brain is constantly on overdrive, and lists help keep any anxiousness, forgetfulness, and disorganization at bay.

- I use lists to organize my thoughts, set goals, keep memories, and learn more about myself.

- I find making lists to be super fun! (Shhh! Don't tell!)

How to Use This Journal

Journaling is an exceptionally beneficial hobby, but it can be a difficult undertaking when you are unsure where to begin. There can be so much beauty in the blank page—all of that potential sitting in front of you, yet no sign of the starting line. Every now and then, we need to be guided in the right direction. We need a little inspiration to push us forward . . . and that's where *My Life in Lists* comes in!

- This journal is comprised of 100 illustrated lists that are ready to inspire and challenge you about your Past, Present, and Future.

- Each page includes a prompt to guide and inspire you. Some pages offer tips and other direction, if needed.

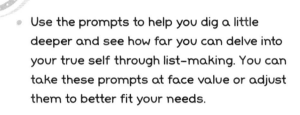

- Use the prompts to help you dig a little deeper and see how far you can delve into your true self through list-making. You can take these prompts at face value or adjust them to better fit your needs.

- These lists cover all aspects of your life, from the simple things to the emotionally complex. This will be a collection of what you have collected—the story of your life through lists.

- There are 5 blank pages in the back of this journal where you can create and illustrate your own lists!

Tips for Getting the Most Out of This Journal

- Use a pencil. Time can change everything from when you first write something down, so use pencil, especially if you see this journal tracking the evolution of your life.

- There are no set rules. You can fill this journal in from cover to cover or you can bounce around and choose the prompts that suit you in the moment.

Adjust to fit your needs. You do not have to fill in every line or box, and you are not limited to the ones provided for you. Above all else, this needs to be functional for YOU!

Swap words for doodles. Try to fill in a page with doodles instead of written responses. Challenge yourself to be creative!

Leave your fear of failure behind. You are human. No one is perfect, and we all make mistakes. If you make a mistake in this book, it's perfectly fine! This is your journal, after all. No judgments!

Lists about Your Past

Achievements

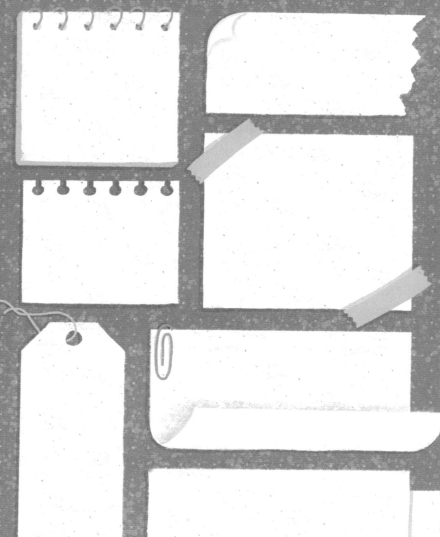

Celebrate your successes! What have you achieved?

Milestones

What moments in your life, big and small, have helped you grow?
List them here

Challenges I've Overcome

Life is full of ups and downs, but every experience truly teaches you something valuable. What are some of the challenges you've overcome in your life?

The Best Advice I Have Ever Received

Favorite Memories

The Best Compliments I Have Ever Received

Dear Past Me . . .

♥ Me

Knowing what you know now, what would you like to tell your past self?

My Most Embarrassing Moments

Time Line of My Life

What significant moments have marked your life and when?

Things That Changed My Life

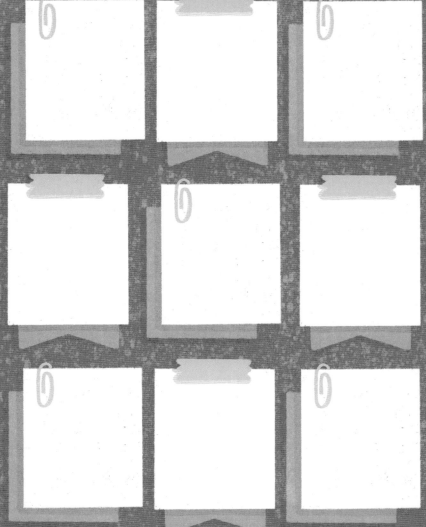

How My Life Has Changed in the Past Year

People Who Changed Me

Some people enter our lives and change us forever.
Who changed your life and why?

Why:

Person:

Why:

Person:

Why:

Person:

Why:

Person:

Person:

Why:

Person:

Why:

Person:

Why:

Person:

Why:

Things That Made Me Laugh

When Did I Last ...

Task	Date	Date	Date

Keep track of your difficult-to-remember reoccurring tasks!
Whether it is a dentist appointment or catching up with a friend, record
the date when you last completed the task to help you stay organized.

The Best
Decisions
I Have Ever Made

Words Used to Describe Me

- ♥
- ♥
- ♥
- ♥
- ♥
- ♥
- ♥
- ♥

Lists for the
Present
You

My Traditions

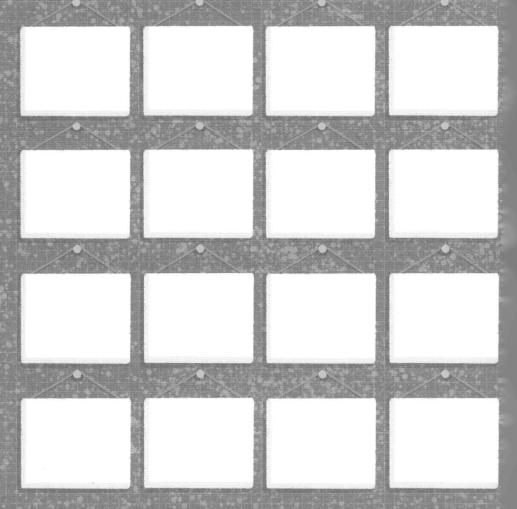

Whether your traditions are with family or friends,
they are worth passing down.
Record them here and keep the traditions alive!

Important Dates and Holidays

JANUARY

FEBRUARY

MARCH

APRIL

MAY

JUNE

JULY

AUGUST

SEPTEMBER

OCTOBER

NOVEMBER

DECEMBER

Brain Bubbles

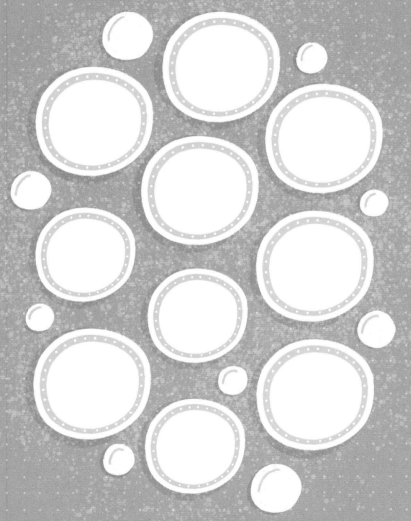

Do you ever have those thoughts that POP into your head,
and then before you know it, they're gone? Jot them down
here before they disappear!

Bright Ideas

Have an idea? Write it down here!
Revisit them from time to time and try
to make these bright ideas a reality.

Check-In

Currently, I am . . .

Reading	Watching	Listening to

Thinking	Feeling	Loving

Disliking	Embracing	Making

15-Minute Me Time

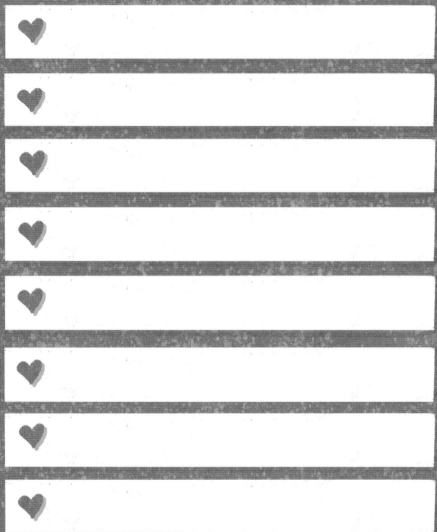

When life becomes overwhelming, take 15 minutes to recharge.
What can you do in 15 minutes that will give you a well-deserved break?

Jot It Down

Use these notepads to make lists!

Dear Diary...

Some things are difficult to say out loud,
so write them down here instead.

Important Birthdays

JANUARY

FEBRUARY

MARCH

APRIL

MAY

JUNE

JULY

AUGUST

SEPTEMBER

OCTOBER

NOVEMBER

DECEMBER

Favorite Websites

Blog

News

Social Media

Shopping

Entertainment

Other

Find Beauty
in the Little Things

Take some time to find beauty in the ordinary. You will be
amazed with what you discover! Record what you find here.

My Fears and How to Conquer Them

Cheer Up, Buttercup!

What cheers you up when you're feeling down?

My Gallery Wall

Creating a gallery wall in your home can be a fabulous way to display your individuality and fill your home with the things you love. How would you show your personality through this gallery wall? You can use motivational words, quotes, and images—it's up to you!

How I Spend My Free Time

I Am Craving . . .

List your favorite foods and drinks here!

I Give Myself Permission to...

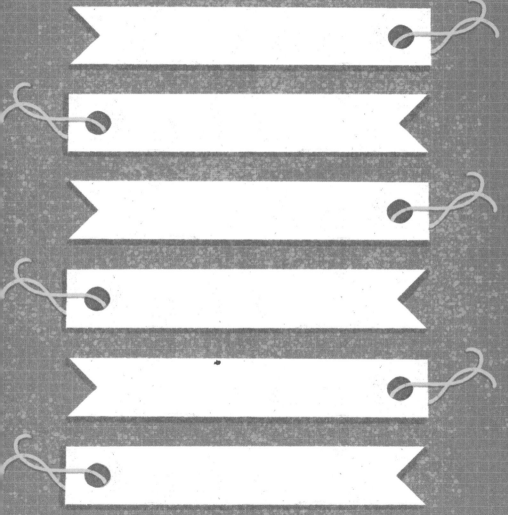

Give yourself permission . . . to be brave . . . to be shy . . . to be imperfect . . .
Allow yourself to be who you are, and you will feel the pressure fade away!

I Am Inspired by...

♥ _____
♥ _____

♥ _____
♥ _____

♥ _____
♥ _____

♥ _____
♥ _____

♥ _____
♥ _____

♥ _____
♥ _____

I Am Most Productive When...

I Am Unique Because ...

-
-
-
-
-
-
-
-

I Am Worried about...

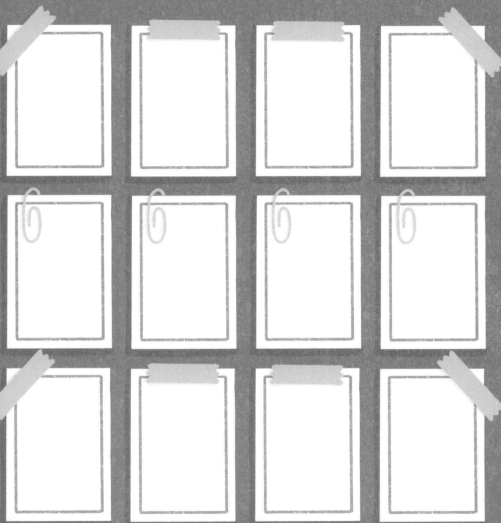

If you are worried about something, jot it down here.
Get it out of your head and onto paper instead!

I Feel Loved When...

I Am Grateful for...

My Hidden Talents

Let those talents shine!

My Favorite Places

Place:

Reason:

Place:

Reason:

Place:

Reason:

Place:

Reason:

Place:

Reason:

Place:

Reason:

Place:

Reason:

Place:

Reason:

Place:

Reason:

A favorite place can be a vacation destination, a restaurant, or even a cozy corner of your home!

My Dream Log

Jot down your dreams on these pillows so you won't lose sleep over it!

My Library

Whether it's favorite books you've read or books you want to read, track them here!

My Priorities Are...

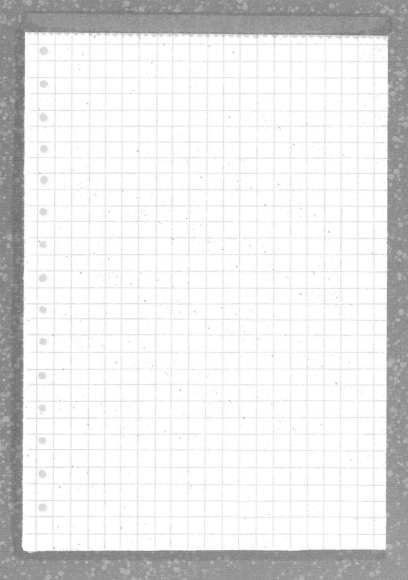

My Quirks Are...

Now Playing

Whether it's favorite
movies you can watch over
and over again or ones you
would like to see, jot them down here.

Movies

People Don't Know That I . . .

What don't people know about you that you would like them to know?

My Un-Do List

You've heard of a to-do list, but here is your UN-DO list—
the things you need to stop doing!

Positive Affirmations

We can be very hard on ourselves every now and then.
Why be your biggest critic when you can be your biggest fan?
Write down positive affirmations and repeat them daily to
remind yourself how incredible and capable you are!

Playlists for Every Mood

Happy Playlist

Sad Playlist

Angry Playlist

Calm Playlist

Self-Care Must-Haves

In today's fast-paced world, it's important to take care of yourself.
What things can you do to practice self-care?

The Soundtrack to My Life

Soundtrack Title:

-
-
-
-
-
-
-
-
-
-
-

If your life was a movie, which songs would be
included on your soundtrack?

What I Am Stressed About
(and How to Relieve It)

Stressful situation:

Steps to take in order to relieve it:
-
-
-
-
-
-

Stressful situation:

Steps to take in order to relieve it:
-
-
-
-
-
-

Stressful situation:

Steps to take in order to relieve it:
-
-
-
-
-

Then | Now

Then	Now
Job	Job
Friends	Friends
Hobby	Hobby
Music	Music
Book	Book
Food	Food
Movie	Movie
TV Show	TV Show
Car	Car

How does your life today compare to a year, two years, or five years ago?

Things I Love to Do

My Unpopular Opinions

Is there something that many people love that you just can't get on board with? Do you love something that other people despise? Write them down here!

Positive Thinking

```
┌─────────────────────────────────────┐
│                                     │
└─────────────────────────────────────┘
```
-
-
-
-
-

```
┌─────────────────────────────────────┐
│                                     │
└─────────────────────────────────────┘
```
-
-
-
-
-

```
┌─────────────────────────────────────┐
│                                     │
└─────────────────────────────────────┘
```
-
-
-
-
-

Choose an existing negative situation and list the positives below it. If you focus on the positives in a situation, you can help change the outcome.

What Is Working

Through trial and error, you can find out what works best for you, and it can be applied to every area of your life. So, what is working for you?

What Isn't Working

Better yourself by taking the time to think about what isn't working in your life. Make changes and you'll see improvement.

Things I Can Control

Things I Can't Control

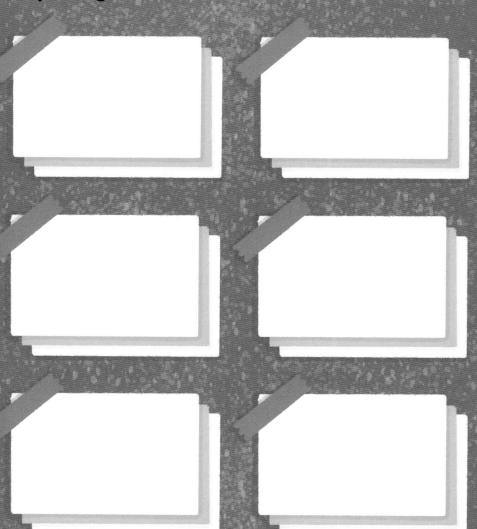

Things That Energize Me

Things That Drain Me

Qualities I Most Admire

★

★

★

★

★

★

★

★

★

★

★

★

Things That Bring Me Joy

Never Have I Ever...

What haven't you done?

What Motivates Me

List the things that push
you to be better!

Things I Collect

What's in My Bag

What you carry with you on a daily basis says a lot about you.
What are your essentials?

Vent It Out!

I Need to Learn to Say No to...

My Professional Skills

Things I Do Well

Lists
to Plan Your
Future

My Short-Term Goals

Which goals would you like to achieve in the next week, month, or year?

My Long-Term Goals

Which goals would you like to achieve in your lifetime?

Lifetime Bucket List

Create your ultimate bucket list and check off each item as you achieve it!

Travel Bucket List

Spring Bucket List

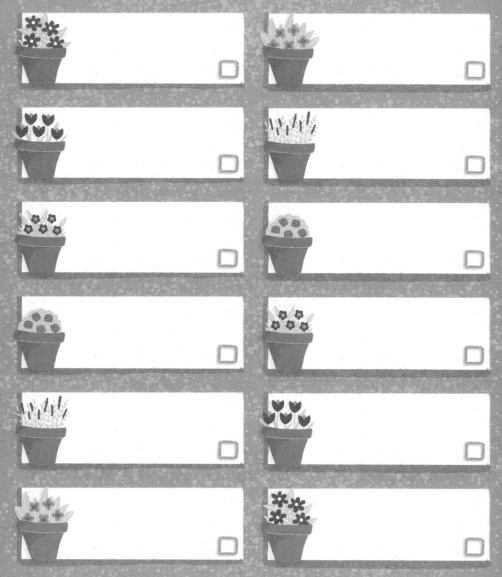

Summer Bucket List

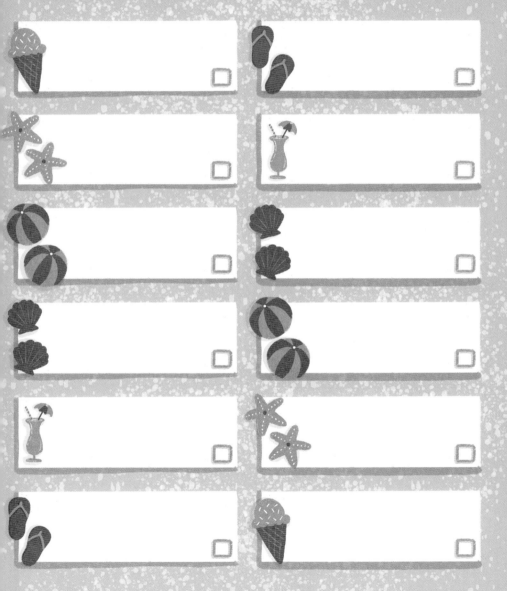

Autumn Bucket List

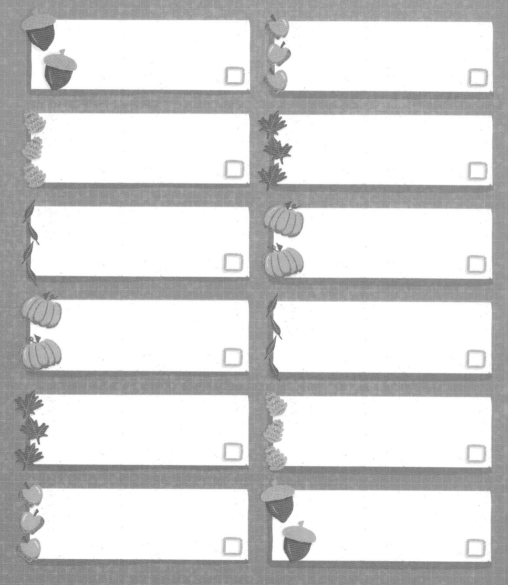

Winter Bucket List

Dear Future Me . . .

Write down what you want to tell your future self.

I Want to Be Known for...

How do you leave your mark on others? Do you want to be known for your compassion? Sense of humor? Creativity? List the things you would like to be known for here.

I Want to Try...

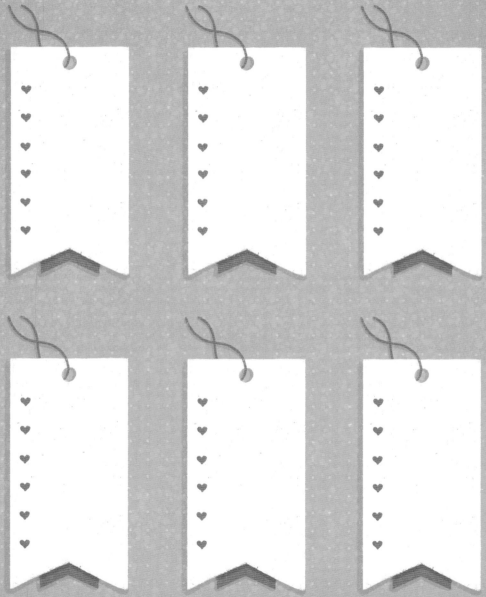

Dream Job

Dreaming of a new job? List your professional ambitions here!

Date Night Ideas

List some fun, creative, and unique plans here!

My Perfect Day

Morning

Afternoon

Night

Declutter List

It's time to declutter! Fill these bags with the things that need your attention and check off their tags when you're done!

My Dream House

Extras:

Room:
- _____
- _____
- _____
- _____
- _____
- _____

Room:
- _____
- _____
- _____
- _____
- _____
- _____

Room:
- _____
- _____
- _____
- _____
- _____

Room:
- _____
- _____
- _____

Room:
- _____
- _____
- _____

Room:
- _____
- _____
- _____
- _____
- _____
- _____

Room:
- _____
- _____
- _____
- _____
- _____
- _____

Room:
- _____
- _____
- _____
- _____
- _____
- _____

If I Won the Lottery, I Would...

Acts of Kindness

One of the biggest gifts you can give others is your kindness.
What can you do for others?

My Vision Board

Welcome to your vision board—an inspirational tool to help you focus on your goals and your future. Add lists, words, quotes, and doodles to help motivate you to achieve your goals!

My Wish List

Have your eye on something special? Write it down here!

I Want to Learn . . .

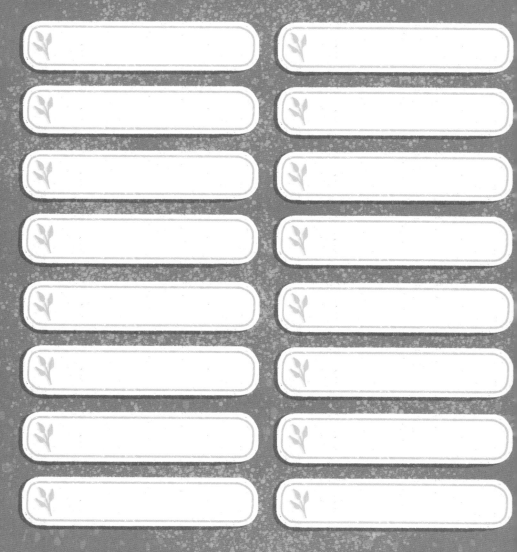

Remember to Research...

Bad Habits...

...I Want to Break

What to Binge-Watch

What television series do you want to binge on? Track them here!

Resolutions

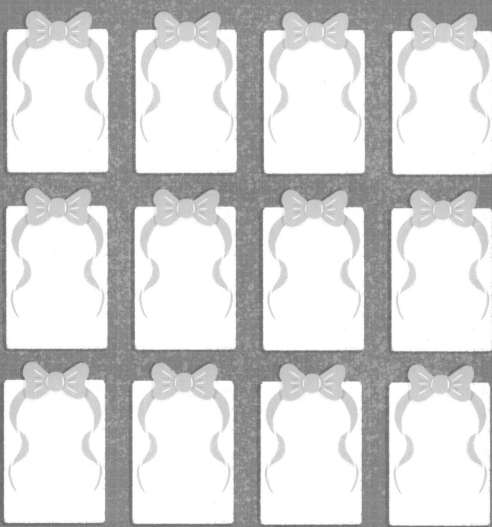

Who says you have to wait until the New Year to make these?

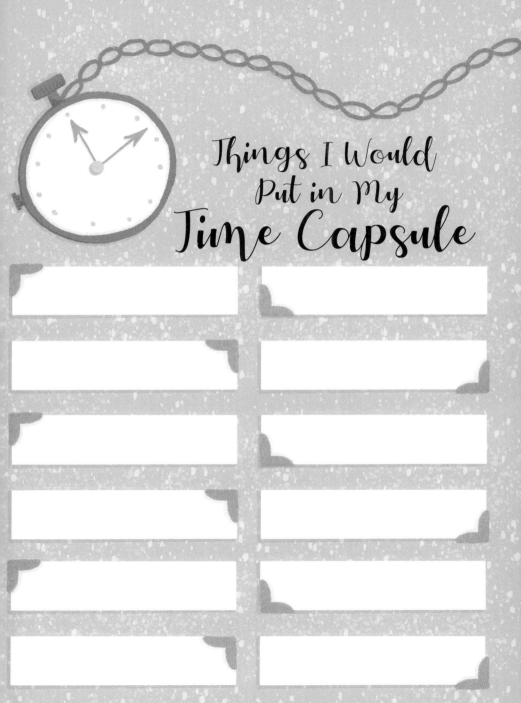

Things I Would Put in My Time Capsule